COPYWRITER'S HANDBOOK :

How To Sell To Anybody And Make Them Prefer You For Life.

Jack Hilton

PUBLIC NOTICE

Despite making every effort to be as precise and thorough as possible, the Publisher does not at any time guarantee or suggest that the contents of this report are correct due to the Internet's tendency to change quickly.

Although every effort has been taken to verify the content in this publication, the Publisher disclaims all liability for any mistakes, omissions, or other interpretations of the subject matter.

Any perceived slights towards particular people, groups, or organizations are accidental.

Like everything else in life, there are no guarantees of income made in books with practical advice. Readers are advised to respond based on their own judgment regarding their own circumstances and take appropriate action.

The goal of this book is not meant to serve as a source of financial, accounting, legal, or

business guidance. We strongly suggest all readers to consult with qualified experts in the disciplines of law, business, accounting, and finance.
This book is recommended for printing for ease of reading.

FOREWORD

Have you ever heard of copywriting? According to Wikipedia, copywriting is the use of words and concepts to advance a person, company, viewpoint, or idea. The term "copywriter" is typically only used in promotional contexts, regardless of the medium (such as in advertisements for print, television, radio, or other media). The word "copy" can be applied to any content intended for printing (such as in the body of a newspaper article or book).

The goal of marketing copy, also known as promotional writing, is to encourage the reader, listener, or spectator to do a particular action, like purchasing a product or endorsing a particular position.

Copywriting is widely utilized in the realm of online marketing to increase blog readership, obtain opt-ins for list building, and generate revenue. If you want to succeed in your online business, you MUST master the art of producing persuasive copy that will win over your audience.

Fortunately, sound copywriting techniques can be learned.

TABLE OF CONTENTS :

CHAPTER 1

The most crucial quality in any marketer is probably their capacity to turn words into gold. If you can accomplish this, it doesn't matter where you are in the world; all it takes is for you to use your words to generate income.

This entire copywriting thing just developed later. The greatest "copywriters" in the past were the renowned businessmen of bygone eras who were adept at selling anything to anyone. People had strong weapons, but their pen (or tongue) was their strongest weapon.

Today's business owners are generating enormous profits by utilizing copywriting strategies. Remember that selling items online is a risk a lot more difficult than selling anything face-to-face because you can't convey sincerity through voice and body LANGUAGE.

However, if you understand how to use the power of copywriting to arouse your customers' emotions, you'll be laughing all the way to the bank.

I'll let you in on these secrets in the following chapters.

CHAPTER 2

COPYWRITING FUNDAMENTALS :

Your online business funnel uses copywriting in many different locations. Here are some instances of frequently visited locations:

What Is BASIC

Content on websites, blogs, landing pages, email marketing, and sales pages
Keep in mind that the ultimate purpose of copywriting is to persuade your readers to take the action you want them to. For instance, completing a purchase or joining your email list.
Therefore, it's crucial that you establish your goal outcome before beginning your copywriting campaign. Precision is knowing what you want before you start writing will

help ensure that your writing goes in the way you intend.

Okay, let's examine some fundamentals.

Considering that we desire for readers to achieve our desired outcome, we also can't be too forceful.

Here is the first guideline:

KEEP IT INFORMAL.

You want to project an image of someone who is authoritative and friendly, not like an obvious salesperson but rather as a thought leader in your field. In the latter scenario, people may hate you or think you're spam.

HEADLINES REQUIREMENTS.

Any copy's headline is the most crucial component. It doesn't matter how strong your offer is or how strong the rest of your text is if your headlines can't pick reader's interest. Make the most of the five seconds you have before your readers scroll past you.

For the title to capture the reader's attention right away, it must be eye-catching and bold. The message of the headline will be strengthened by the subheadline.
In this instance, the author employed the "Impact" font face and red fonts to grab the interest of the reader. The black lettering in the header serve to break up the headline's monotony. Additionally, it is employed to highlight crucial points (Free Of Charge) (Free Of Charge).

A crucial point to remember is that your headline should never be written in ALL CAPS. Use it just as required.

Imagine how this would appear if it were at the top of your website. Who would want to hear someone yelling at them, it seems?

Full caps also appear spammy, and neither Google nor anyone else would enjoy that.

Additionally, catchy words that may rapidly arouse emotions must be included in headlines. Do magazines ever appear on newsstands?

The headlines typically have captivating language and exciting words, curiosity and feelings when discussing matters like money, drama, and sex.

What industry or niche do you fit into? What terms can you use in your niche to stir up feelings and drama?

CHAPTER 3

ESP versus USP :

In the previous chapter, we covered emotions in great detail. In the past, numerous companies used "unique selling points" or "unique selling propositions" to set themselves apart from their rivals and increase sales.

While that is crucial, in the internet world, we also have something else termed a "Emotional Selling Point" (ESP), which is the capacity to appeal to readers' emotions in order to persuade them to do the required action.

An illustration of an emotional selling pitch is this:
"I had experienced the hardships of being a novice marketer learning how to drive traffic to my website. Due to the fact that my Web

business wasn't producing much revenue, I occasionally even had one slice of bread every day.

This timeless illustration connects the marketer's struggles to the reader of the sales copy, who probably has similar difficulties today.

Strong emotion-stimulating words are frequently used in emotional selling pitches. For instance, you may use phrases like "time and financial independence, free from the chains of the 9-5, quit the rat face" in the make money online area. These phrases, which relate to the market niche in which people can simply put.

If you want to effectively sell your company with ESPs, consider these two issues:

1) What market do you serve?
2) What phrases, narratives, or circumstances can your target audience relate to?

Once you know the answers to these two questions, you can try to come up with as many ESPs as you can to use in your marketing or sales copy.

CHAPTER 4

One of the most important elements of any piece of content is the call to action. Determine what is your most desired outcome for your clients or potential customers before doing anything else.

Action typically in different parts of your organization would call for various kinds of desired results. Comments on a blog, Likes on a Facebook page, Opt-in landing pages, Email clickthrough rates, Purchases from sales pages, etc. These are the normal outcomes that you would seek. Therefore, once you've made that decision, you must formulate your call to action or design to make that kind of action easier. For instance, "If you liked this post or have any suggestions of your own, please comment down below!" would be a terrific call to action for a blog. Even while it may seem absurd to advise a reader exactly what to do, split test studies have proven that this is actually very effective. The greatest method to get results quickly is to copy what others have done and stop doing things that don't work.

Another illustration: If you want potential customers to buy from you, you may tell them to "Snap up your copy before it runs out!"
A straightforward scarcity component has been included as one of the extra marketing nuggets (frequently used) by warning that if you don't act now, it will run out.

Don't forget to incorporate it in whatever you do because adding time restrictions or scarcity variables to your call to actions frequently results in high conversions.
Last but not least, keep in mind that the effectiveness of the call to action depends not only on the language used, but also on

how you combine various elements of your sales pitch, such as ESPs, how you respond to objections, and how you highlight the benefits.

CHAPTER 5

MANAGING REBUTTALS :

An essential component of effective sales copywriting is handling objections.
Every time someone reads a piece of sales copy, numerous concerns "guard" him from "losing his money" come to mind. This is a normal habit, and if you can deal with these concerns in your text as they arise, you will reap great benefits.

Here are a few methods frequently employed for handling objections:

1) REFERENCES
Almost everyone searches for social proof when making a purchasing decision.

They will be more convinced that the product is good if the testimonial appears more convincing and real. Try to incorporate testimonials with customer photos, or even better, use video testimonials.

2) FAQS

A commonly asked questions area is quite helpful in dispelling any doubts that may arise. Here, you can address all of the frequently held misconceptions that might surface, including questions about how to use the product, who it is best suited for, and price issues.

3) POST SCRIPTS (P.S)

Postscripts, often known as P.S., are frequently used in sales letters to increase conversions. People typically have a last line of defense before pressing the "Add to cart" button, preventing them from the acquisition. You can give them the final push to make the purchase if you have a few post scripts prepared.

4) REASONS TO PURCHASE

This piece, which is a personal favorite of mine, provides your readers with a few compelling arguments to support their purchase and significantly increase your revenues.

Your sales will quickly skyrocket if you include these fantastic strategies for addressing objections in your sales text!

CHAPTER 6

AVOID THESE COPYWRITING MISTAKES:

In their marketing careers, everyone makes errors. This section seeks to guide you past the entire "experimental phase" and steer clear of the biggest copywriting gaffes ever.

1. Selling without first demonstrating value is mistake number one. Always provide your subscribers with tons of free value and build sincere relationships with them before bombarding them with offers.

2. Incorrect text alignment – As a general guideline, words should always be aligned to the left, slightly indented inside, and with a word line that is not excessively long. Here is to

avoid having the flow of your visitor's reading stop. (moving right to left) Additionally, photos should only be used rarely and only be centered if they are directly related to your sales copy.

3. Sounding overly formal. It's a fact that if your pitch sound is too professional, you'll come across as a robotic salesperson. Please, add some human interest and speak in a relaxed manner. Nobody wants to be pressured into buying, so you'll have a better chance of closing the deal if you can relate to your readers on a more casual level and help them identify with you.

4. Wasting the time of your readers for the most part, you should only add elements that support the sale and eliminate those that do not. Your reader's attention is incredibly

valuable, so if you do manage to capture it, make the most of it. Avoid boring them with pointless talk.

If you stay away from these blunders and actively practice the copywriting techniques described above, you'll quickly improve and generate more sales.

If You Follow My Proven Steps, There's No Way You Can't Make Money Copying My Proven System!

Find your passions and use your innate talent to make these into a career.

Learn the wealth-generating formula kept secret until now by only the top Internet millionaires... OR

sitting at home doing nothing to advance wealth creation. The life's work is your business engine! Numerous individuals throughout the world earn money online using a computer and a few hours each week! Are you willing to work hard for a huge online income?

Have the 9–5 hours gotten old to you? How Concerning Is the Financial Crisis?

If so, you're in to join a team that will take on any challenge for the cost of a quick takeout all the way to monetary achievement!

An amazing quick, simple, and cheap method to earn a ton of extra money and get a ton of exposure while you sleep!

Making Money From Home Has Never Been Simpler! You've just started a mission that can't possibly fail.

In Conclusion...

It takes skill to be able to sell with your words and generate enormous revenues.
Thank goodness, it's also a skill that can be developed. As a marketer, it is your responsibility to consistently use these techniques every day. The more copies you produce, the better you'll become over time.

You'll have no trouble producing our top-notch sales copies. If your sales text doesn't convert well, don't become discouraged. Keep tweaking your copy and remove the things that don't work and replace them with alternatives that do work.

You become faster as you become better. having more free time to increase revenue, you can concentrate on other aspects of your firm.

Congratulations!
Gain For Yourself!